GUIDE TO
Marine Mammals
of Alaska

Fourth Edition

by Kate Wynne
Illustrated by Pieter Folkens

Sea Grant

MAB-44
Price: $25.00

Alaska Sea Grant
University of Alaska Fairbanks
Fairbanks, AK 99775-5040
(888) 789-0090
Fax (907) 474-6285
alaskaseagrant.org

Author Biography

Since 1981, Kate Wynne has been involved in assessing marine mammal populations and their interactions with commercial fisheries. Her studies include the survey, capture, and necropsy of more than twelve species of marine mammals in New England and Alaska, including cetaceans, pinnipeds, and sea otters. She has worked eight years as a marine mammal observer, has designed and coordinated marine mammal observer programs, and continues to train fishery observers in mammal identification. She earned her master's degree in wildlife management from the University of Maine, and currently is professor of marine biology at the University of Alaska Fairbanks.

As marine mammal specialist for the Alaska Sea Grant Marine Advisory Program in Kodiak, one of Wynne's missions is to provide information for understanding and complying with complex and changing marine mammal laws. She believes that informed and cooperative resource users are vital to collecting reliable scientific data about marine resources—including mammals. Her research experience and her contact with fishermen, biologists, and observers inspired her to provide this book to help identify marine mammals in Alaska.

Acknowledgments

Enthusiastic support of this publication is testimony to the communal concern for and appreciation of the marine mammal resources of Alaska.

Funding was provided by the National Marine Fisheries Service, Office of Protected Resources, Silver Spring, MD; U.S. Fish and Wildlife Service, Marine Mammals Management, Anchorage, AK; Pacific States Marine Fisheries Commission, Portland, OR; and Marine Mammal Commission, Washington, DC.

Original species account reviewers were Marilyn Dahlheim, Tony DeGange, Rich Ferrero, Charles Fowler, Kathy Frost, Pat Gearin, Camille Goebel-Diaz, Harriet Huber, Brendan Kelly, Tom Loughlin, Dale Rice, David Rugh, Scott Schliebe, Dana Seagars, John Sease, Ward Testa, David Withrow, and Allen Wolman. A special thanks to Carrie LeDuc, Kathy Frost, and Jon Nickles for reviewing the final drafts of this guide.

As our climate continues to change, we will likely see shifts in species' distribution. Future editions will incorporate sightings/updates submitted by users of this guide.

Table of Contents

Marine mammals have captured public interest as unique, intelligent, and sometimes competitive marine inhabitants. They have played an integral role in Native Alaskan culture for thousands of years, providing food, shelter, clothing, and handicrafts for coastal residents. In the United States, marine mammals have been federally protected since passage of the Marine Mammal Protection Act of 1972 and have gained popularity among marine recreationists and the general public. Drastic increases and decreases in some marine mammal populations have generated recent concern among marine resource users, biologists, and managers about the health of marine ecosystems and effects of human interactions with marine mammals. Arctic and coastal development pose increasing threats of disturbance, mortality, and oil contamination.

While marine mammal viewing and species identification remain a popular form of recreation, some federal species-specific regulations now require accurate identification of marine mammals. Commercial fishermen are required to identify marine mammals and report the species that interact with their gear. Federal marine resource observers are trained to identify marine mammals seen while monitoring commercial fishing operations. Even whale-watching vessels and tour boats now must follow federal guidelines when approaching whales.

This guide was inspired by the needs and desires of the diverse marine resource users who share Alaska's waters with marine mammals. It is designed to familiarize the observer with marine mammal characteristics and present species descriptions in a format that encourages fast, accurate identification at sea. It is intended to be informative yet readable, complete yet brief, and equally useful in a fisherman's wheelhouse, tour boat stateroom, or biologist's backpack. The book is printed on water resistant paper so that it will withstand hard wear and wet conditions.

The geographic scope of this guide has been limited to allow fast field identification of the nearly 30 Alaska species. We acknowledge the world distribution of each species but focus on their approximate distribution in waters surrounding Alaska: the North Pacific Ocean (including the Gulf of Alaska and Bering Sea) and the Arctic Ocean (including the Chukchi and Beaufort seas). A map of the area covered by this book is on the inside back cover.

For information on reporting a stranded or entangled marine mammal, please see http://bit.ly/2fhVqia.

Using This Book to Identify Marine Mammals

Accurate identification of marine mammals at sea often requires rapid incorporation of many clues during brief and distant visual contact. The physical traits, location (geographic and local habitat), and behavior of the animal are all important clues to note when viewing marine mammals and differentiating similar species. Tips:

1. Know what characteristics to look for. Review guides prior to your trip, and know what features are most helpful in species identification.

2. Be patient and persistent. Continue scanning the area—it may be several minutes before a marine mammal resurfaces.

3. Don't lose observation time thumbing through a field guide. Keep your eye on the mammal and make mental notes or quick sketches of key traits for later comparison with guides.

4. Don't jump to conclusions. Some marine mammal behavior is misleading. Pinnipeds and sea otters often break the surface (porpoise) while swimming fast, and several cetaceans sleep motionless at the surface. Continue observing to verify identification. Never base identification on behavior alone. Have at least two physical characteristics to make a positive identification.

5. This guide is specifically designed to aid accurate identification of mammals at sea.

   - Color-coded sections separate cetaceans and pinnipeds from other marine mammals.

   - Composite diagrams of species drawn to scale allow size and trait comparisons at a glance.

   - Gender identification and morphological traits are illustrated.

   - Species are grouped by family and presented in descending order by adult size.

- Range maps show generalized seasonal distribution of each species: pink = summer, blue = winter, purple = year-round.

- **Key characteristics** are presented in **bold** text.

- Silhouette surface profiles accentuate traits visible at sea under poor light conditions.

- Silhouette profiles are presented for direct comparison of species with similar traits and distribution.

- Glossary on page 72 defines terms used in the text.

Mammals are animals that breathe air through lungs, are warm-blooded, have hair (at some time during life), bear young alive, and suckle their young.

Marine mammals are a diverse group thought to have evolved from terrestrial ancestors to aquatic life through a number of unique physical adaptations. Representatives are found in every ocean, on every continent, and in a variety of ecological roles, including herbivores (manatees), filter feeders (baleen whales), and apex predators (killer whales).

In this book we present three groups of Alaska marine mammals in order from most to least aquatic specialization: cetaceans (whales, dolphins, and porpoises), pinnipeds (seals, sea lions, and walrus), and marine fissipeds (sea otter and polar bear).

Cetaceans and pinnipeds exhibit extraordinary anatomical and physiological adaptations to a marine existence. Consider the physical demands on a warm-blooded, air-breathing animal living an amphibious or totally marine existence. Marine mammals have adapted to the extreme temperatures, depths, pressure, darkness, and density of the medium they live in.

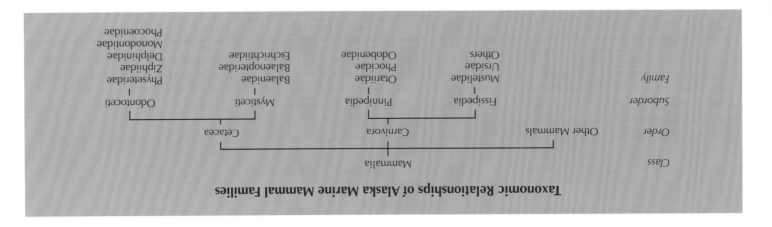

Taxonomic Relationships of Alaska Marine Mammal Families

Class	Order	Suborder	Family
Mammalia	Cetacea	Odontoceti	Physeteridae, Ziphiidae, Delphinidae, Monodontidae, Phocoenidae
		Mysticeti	Balaenidae, Balaenopteridae, Eschrichtiidae
	Carnivora	Pinnipedia	Otariidae, Phocidae, Odobenidae
		Fissipedia	Mustelidae, Ursidae, Others
	Other Mammals		

Marine Adaptations

Deep Diving

Generally, their lungs are proportionately smaller than humans' but marine mammals:

- Use oxygen more efficiently. They fill their lungs and exchange 90% of their air in each breath, have high blood volume, and their blood chemistry allows greater oxygen retention (the high red blood cell count and increased myoglobin make their muscle tissue and blood dark red).

Kate Wynne

- Have a high tolerance to lactic acid and carbon dioxide. Their muscles can work anaerobically (without oxygen) while they hold their breath.
- Can tolerate tremendous atmospheric pressure at great depths. Lungs and ribs are collapsible, air spaces are minimized, and nitrogen absorption is limited.

Swimming Adaptations

- Drag is reduced by hydrodynamic body forms.
- Appendages are modified for maximal propulsion and minimal drag.

Thermoregulation

- A large body with small surface to volume ratio reduces heat loss. Blubber or thick underfur is used as insulation.

Marine mammals, such as this harbor seal, have streamlined bodies with modified appendages that increase their swimming ◀ and thermal efficiency.

- Complex circulatory system in extremities is used to conserve and dissipate heat.
- Young pinnipeds and cetaceans grow fast on milk with 40-50% fat (human milk is 3.3% fat).

Water Conservation

Most marine mammals rarely drink fresh water; instead they:

- Utilize water present in their food, inspired air, and blubber.
- Have specialized kidneys which produce urine that is saltier than sea water.

Sensory Adaptations

Marine mammals communicate under water with sound and many species use sound (echolocation) to locate prey. Tactile senses are acute. Pinnipeds and fissipeds have well-developed facial whiskers.

Cetaceans are completely aquatic mammals: they feed, mate, calve, and suckle their young in the water. They are the most specialized mammalian swimmers. Some are capable of maintaining speeds up to 25 mph, diving to depths to 10,000 ft, and remaining submerged up to 2 hrs. The body is streamlined (limbs are tapered or lacking) and the tail is developed into horizontal flukes for propulsion. The smooth, supple, and hairless skin further reduces drag during swimming.

Cetaceans breathe through nostrils (blowhole) on top of the head. When surfacing after a dive, whales forcefully expel the previous lungful of air (blow) and inspire new air. Characteristics of the blow are useful for identification.

Cetaceans are grouped into two taxonomic suborders: the baleen whales (Mysticeti) and the toothed whales (Odontoceti). Mysticetes are filterfeeders that forage for zooplankton and small fish by skimming or gulping huge amounts of prey and water. The water is then forced back out the mouth past hundreds of baleen plates that act as sieves to trap the prey, which is then swallowed.

Odontocetes have various numbers of identical conical or spade-shaped teeth that are used to strain or grasp prey, primarily fish and squid.

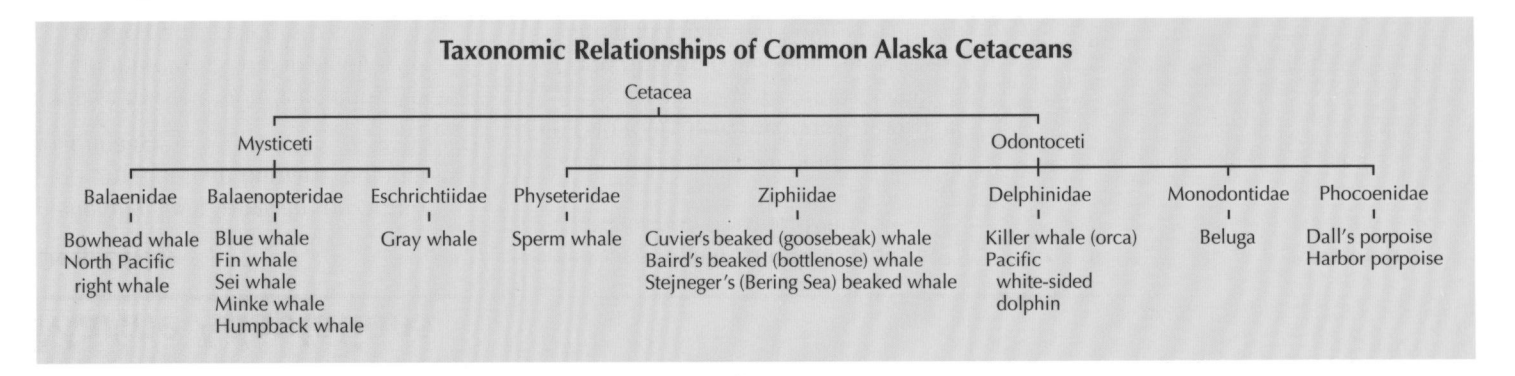

Taxonomic Relationships of Common Alaska Cetaceans

Mysticetes (Baleen Whales)

All mysticetes have two nostrils. Females are generally larger than males but otherwise there is no sexual dimorphism. They are not known to echolocate prey. All three families are found in Alaska waters.

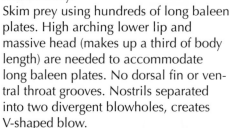

Balaenidae (Right whales): Robust body. Skim prey using hundreds of long baleen plates. High arching lower lip and massive head (makes up a third of body length) are needed to accommodate long baleen plates. No dorsal fin or ventral throat grooves. Nostrils separated into two divergent blowholes, creates V-shaped blow.

Balaenopteridae (Rorquals): Numerous ventral throat grooves allow expansion for large-volume gulping of prey and water. Dorsal fin present. Single, straight blow.

Eschrichtiidae (Gray whale): Skim or dredge mud for crustaceans. Robust body with no dorsal fin or ventral throat grooves. Two to seven short, deep creases on throat. Baleen short and yellow.

Odontocetes (Toothed Whales)

All odontocetes have a single nostril blowhole. Sexual dimorphism is common—males are larger than females, and diagnostic secondary sex traits are present in some families (differences in dorsal fins, tooth pattern). Echolocation for prey is common. Five families are found in Alaska.

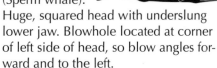

Physeteridae (Sperm whale): Huge, squared head with underslung lower jaw. Blowhole located at corner of left side of head, so blow angles forward and to the left.

Ziphiidae (Beaked whales): Various degrees of beak and dorsal fin development. Deep, long divers.

Delphinidae (Dolphins): Beak present. Prominent central dorsal fin; variable melon. Conical teeth. Shallow divers.

Monodontidae (Beluga): No dorsal fin. Prominent melon.

Phocoenidae (Porpoises): No beak. Dorsal fin present. Spade-shaped teeth.

Note: Figures on this page show general body shapes. The whales are not drawn to scale.

Morphology of Cetaceans

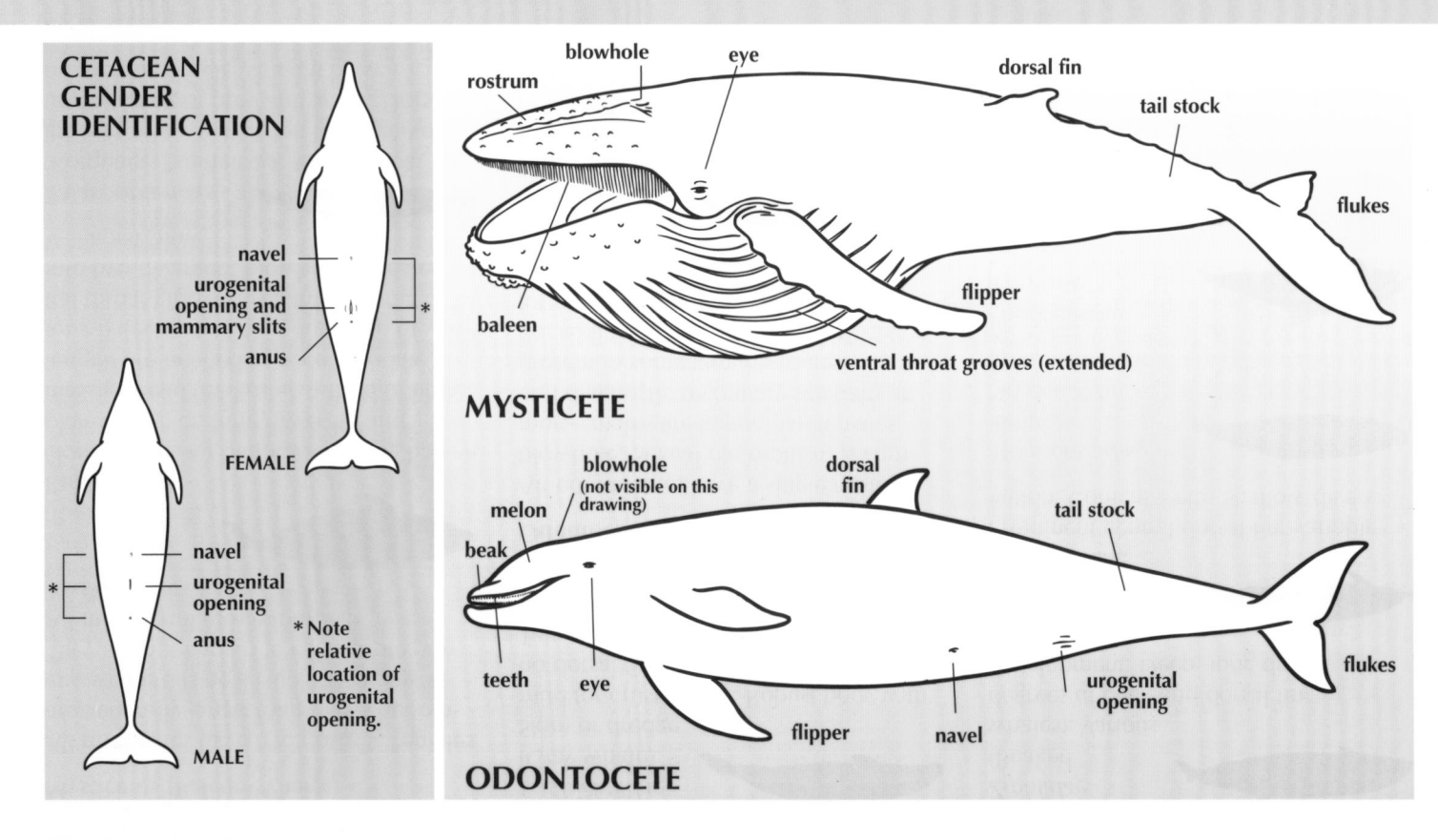

CETACEAN GENDER IDENTIFICATION

navel

urogenital opening and mammary slits

anus

*

FEMALE

navel

urogenital opening

anus

*

MALE

*Note relative location of urogenital opening.

blowhole

rostrum

eye

dorsal fin

tail stock

flukes

baleen

flipper

ventral throat grooves (extended)

MYSTICETE

blowhole (not visible on this drawing)

melon

beak

dorsal fin

tail stock

teeth

eye

flipper

navel

urogenital opening

flukes

ODONTOCETE

Gray Whale

Bowhead Whale

Harbor Porpoise

Dall's Porpoise

Pacific White-Sided Dolphin

Sei Whale

Stejneger's Beaked Whale

Right Whale

Killer Whale

Minke Whale

Fin Whale

Baird's Beaked Whale

Blue Whale

Cuvier's Beaked Whale

Humpback Whale

Beluga

Sperm Whale

Common Cetaceans of Alaska

feet	0	5	10	15	20	25	30

| meters | 0 | 1 | 2 | 3 | 4 | 5 | 6 | 7 | 8 | 9 | 10 |

Bowhead Whale

Balaena mysticetus   Family: Balaenidae

Pieter Folkens

SIZE: Max 60 ft (18 m), max wt 75 tons. Length at birth 10-15 ft (3-4.5 m).

BODY: Robust body with **smooth skin;** massive head with **raised blowhole.** High arching upper jaws hold up to 350 dark baleen plates per side, each to 12 ft (3.6 m) long. Bowed lower lips enfold a narrow rostrum. Flippers short and spatulate. **Lacks callosities.**

COLOR: Predominantly black with **white chin patch.** Some have white on tail stock.

DORSAL FIN: No dorsal fin. Back smooth.

BLOW: V-shaped, bushy, to 18 ft (5.5 m) high.

BEHAVIOR: Slow swimmers. Can break through 1-2 ft thick ice with head. Usually single or groups of ≤3 but aggregations of 50-60 may occur on feeding grounds. Highly vocal during migration.

DIVE PATTERN: Dive duration 15-20 min. Surface interval is 3-5 min.

Bowhead Whale

Fluke   Back   Blow

CAN BE CONFUSED WITH:

North Pacific Right Whale

H. Braham

Note smooth back, raised blowhole,
v-shaped blow, and white lower lip.

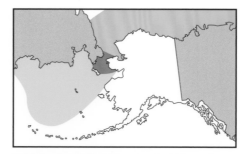

Distribution/Migration: Arctic. Winter in Bering Sea and follow leads in ice n. to summer feeding grounds in Chukchi and Beaufort seas. Often seen migrating n. with belugas.

Dave Withrow, NOAA Fisheries, NMML

This view from top of harvested bowhead shows long, fringed baleen plates extending from rostrum.

HABITAT: Rarely far from ice.

FOOD HABITS: Zooplankton specialists. Prey on small to medium size copepods, euphausiids, amphipods. Skim through large schools with mouth agape. May eat up to 3000 lbs per day.

LIFE HISTORY: Sexually mature at 12-20 yrs. Female has 1 calf every 3-7 yrs. Single calves born Apr-May after gestation of 12-16 mos. Lactation lasts about 1 yr. May live well over 100 yrs.

STATUS AND HUMAN INTERACTIONS: Endangered but increasing. Approx 12,000 in Bering, Chukchi, and Beaufort seas. AK Native subsistence hunters land 35-50 per year. Noise from offshore oil activities has potential impact on migrating bowheads.

Bowhead Whale

Balaena mysticetus
Family: Balaenidae

SIZE: Max length 56 ft (17 m), avg wt 60 tons. Females larger than males. Length at birth 15-20 ft (4.6-6 m).

BODY: Robust body with large head (one fourth body length). Bowed lower lips enfold narrow, arching rostrum. **Callosities** (wart-like growths) on the rostrum, lower lip, and around the eyes. Up to 250 dark baleen plates per side, each to 9 ft (2.8 m) long. Flippers broad and spatulate. Wide flukes with smooth edges and deep notch.

COLOR: Predominantly black, some white patches on belly.

DORSAL FIN: No dorsal fin.

BLOW: V-shaped, bushy, to 16 ft (5 m) high.

BEHAVIOR: Docile. Slow swimmers but are more acrobatic than bowheads (often breaching, flipper slapping). Vocalization is variety of moans and burps.

DIVE PATTERN: Blow 5-10 times at 15-30 sec intervals, then dive for 5-15 min. Usually show flukes before deep dives.

Pieter Folkens

North Pacific Right Whale

Fluke   Back   Blow

CAN BE CONFUSED WITH:

Bowhead Whale

John Durban, NMFS

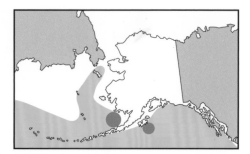

Distribution/Migration: N. Hemisphere. Migratory patterns are unclear. Historically, s. Bering Sea and Gulf of AK were primary summer range. May winter as far s. as Baja California. Circles show areas with recent repeated sightings.

Note: All photo-documented right whale sightings in North Pacific waters are of great value to whale researchers!

Note the bonnet of callosities on high-arching rostrum and lower lip on the North Pacific right whale.

HABITAT: Mostly temperate and subpolar waters. Calving may occur in shallow bays and coastal waters.

FOOD HABITS: Zooplankton specialists: primary prey is euphausiids and copepods, gathered by skimming through schools with mouth agape.

LIFE HISTORY: Uncertain but probably breed in winter-spring at low latitudes and calve the following winter after gestation of 12 months. Single calf every 2-4 yrs. Lactation lasts 1 yr.

STATUS AND HUMAN INTERACTIONS: Critically endangered. Populations were decimated by commercial whalers who named it the right whale because it is easily approached, floats when killed, and is rich in oil. Completely protected in U.S. waters since 1967 but population remains critically low (probably <100). A sighting of 17 right whales in w. Bristol Bay in July 2004 included a female and 2 calves.

North Pacific Right Whale

Eubalaena japonica
Family: Balaenidae

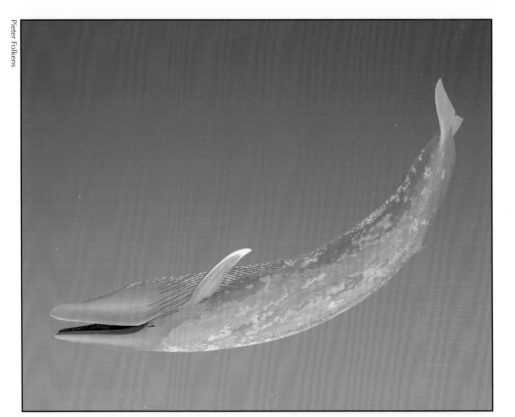

Pieter Folkens

SIZE: Avg adult 85 ft (26 m), 100 tons. At birth 23 ft (7 m), 5500 lbs. Earth's largest animal ever.

BODY: Huge, sleek body. **Broad, flat, U-shaped rostrum** (when viewed from above) with up to 400 broad, black, 3 ft long (1 m) baleen plates per side. Flippers long, slender, pointed. Flukes broad with notched, straight trailing edge. 55-68 ventral throat grooves.

COLOR: Body **blue-gray** with light **mottling.** Tongue, palate, and **baleen black.**

DORSAL FIN: Small (1 ft high), variable shape, **located far aft** (three-fourths head-tail distance), and often not seen until diving.

BLOW: Dense (not bushy), vertical blow to 30 ft (9 m) high.

BEHAVIOR: Travel alone or in pairs. Fast swimmers (bursts of up to 20 knots).

DIVE PATTERN: 1 blow every 1-2 min. Normal dive is 3-10 min, max is 30 min. **May raise flukes slightly.**

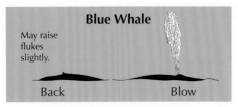

Blue Whale

May raise flukes slightly.

Back   Blow

CAN BE CONFUSED WITH:

Fin Whale

▲ Tiny dorsal fin is far aft on huge, mottled, light blue back of the blue whale.

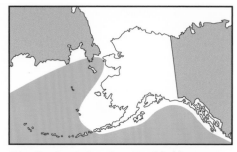

Sally Mizroch

Distribution/Migration: Worldwide. In N. Pacific, migrate to summer feeding grounds from CA n. into e. Gulf of AK, along Aleutians, and into Bering Sea. Migrate s. to wintering-calving grounds 1-10°N.

Gerry Joyce

◄ Note broad flat rostrum, open nostrils, and mottled back of blue whale.

HABITAT: Pelagic but may use deep coastal waters.

FOOD HABITS: Specialists. Eat primarily euphausiids. May fast much of winter but consume estimated 4 tons per day during peak summer feeding periods.

LIFE HISTORY: Sexually mature at 10 yrs. Breed in fall and winter. Single calf every 2-3 yrs after gestation of 12 mos. Lactation lasts 7 mos. Calves gain 200 lbs per day (or 8 lbs per hr). May live 80 yrs.

STATUS AND HUMAN INTERACTIONS: Endangered. Estimated 8000-9000 worldwide, 1200-1700 in eastern N. Pacific. Rare in Alaska. Commercially overharvested but completely protected in U.S. since 1965. Vessel collisions and man-made noise are potential threats.

Blue Whale

Balaenoptera musculus
Family: Balaenopteridae

SIZE: Adults 50-80 ft (17-24 m), 70 tons. Females larger than males. At birth 21 ft (6.5 m), 2 tons.

BODY: Large sleek body. Rostrum **V-shaped** and flat with up to 475 two ft long (0.7 m) gray or white baleen plates per side. 55-100 ventral throat grooves. **Distinct ridge** on back from dorsal fin to **broad triangular flukes.**

COLOR: Dark gray with light undersides, **pale chevron** on dorsal neck surface. Asymmetrical jaw coloration: lower **right jaw white** but left **jaw dark.**

DORSAL FIN: Up to 2 ft tall, falcate with blunt tip, swept back at low angle, located two-thirds distance between head and tail. **Appears shortly after blow.**

BLOW: Tall, elliptical, 18-20 ft (6 m) high.

BEHAVIOR: Often seen in groups of 6-10, alone or in pairs. Fast swimmers (bursts to 20 mph).

Pieter Folkens

Lower right jaw is white

Lower left jaw is dark

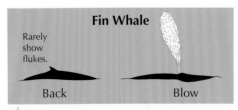

Fin Whale

Rarely show flukes.

Back   Blow

CAN BE CONFUSED WITH:

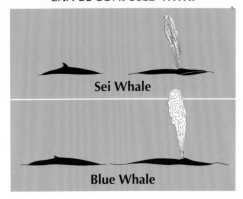

Sei Whale

Blue Whale

Note low angle of fin whale's blunt dorsal fin. ▶

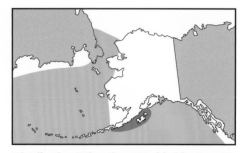

Distribution/Migration: Worldwide. In e. N. Pacific, winter from central CA s., migrate n. as far as Chukchi Sea to summer feeding grounds in Gulf of AK, Prince William Sound, along Aleutians. Some are found yr-round in w. Gulf of Alaska.

UAF/GAP, Permit 1049-1718

DIVE PATTERN: Rarely show flukes. Produce 4-8 blows at 10-20 sec intervals, then dive for 5-15 min. Max depth is 1000 ft (300 m).

HABITAT: Generally pelagic but may use deep coastal waters.

FOOD HABITS: Generalists. Prey on variety of small schooling fish and invertebrates by gulping large swarms while swimming on side. Feed primarily in summer.

LIFE HISTORY: Sexually mature at 6-12 yrs. Breed in winter. Single calf every 2+ yrs born in winter after gestation of 11-12 mos. Lactation lasts 6 mos. May live 100 yrs.

STATUS AND HUMAN INTERACTIONS: Endangered. Population estimate: 75,000 worldwide. 16,000 in e. N. Pacific. Commercially harvested in N. Pacific until 1976. Vessel collisions and man-made noise are potential threats.

Fin Whale

Pieter Folkens

SIZE: Avg adult male 46 ft (14 m), 25 tons. Avg adult female 49 ft (15 m), 30 tons. At birth 15 ft (4.5 m), 1 ton.

BODY: Sleek dark body with down-turned pointed rostrum. Up to 400 2.7 ft long (0.8 m) dark baleen plates per side. Flippers slender and pointed. Large, notched flukes. 32-60 **short ventral throat grooves.**

COLOR: Dark gray with pale belly. Frequent light mottling and patches. **Both lower lips gray.**

DORSAL FIN: Prominent, erect, falcate, about 2 ft high and located two-thirds distance between head and tail. **Often visible with blow.**

BLOW: Elliptical, to 10 ft (3 m) high. Similar in shape but shorter than fin whale's blow.

BEHAVIOR: Fastest swimming baleen whale (to 20 knots). Commonly seen alone or in groups of 2-5.

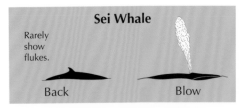

Sei Whale

Rarely show flukes.

Back

Blow

CAN BE CONFUSED WITH:

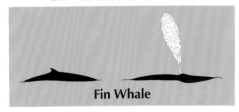

Fin Whale

Note erect, strongly falcate dorsal fin on sei whale. ▶

Distribution/Migration: Worldwide. Migrate between high-latitude summer feeding grounds and low-latitude winter breeding grounds. In e. N. Pacific, spend summers from CA to Gulf of AK and winters from central CA south, possibly to equator.

Cornelia Oedekoven, courtesy NOAA SFSC

DIVE PATTERN: Break surface with tip of rostrum. Back remains visible longer than for other large whales, then **dorsal fin sinks slowly straight down rather than wheeling forward like fin whale.** Blow 2-6 times between dives of 5-30 min. **Seldom arch back or show flukes when diving.**

HABITAT: Pelagic.

FOOD HABITS: Generalists. Skim through schools of crustaceans (mainly copepods but also amphipods, euphausiids), small fish, and squid. May eat 1 ton per day.

LIFE HISTORY: Sexually mature at 10 yrs. Breed mostly in winter. Single calf every 3 yrs after gestation of 11.5-12 mos. Lactation lasts 6-9 mos. May live 60 yrs.

STATUS AND HUMAN INTERACTIONS: Endangered. Commercially harvested in N. Pacific until 1986 for meat and oil but now protected and estimated at 14,000. Vessel collisions and man-made noise are potential threats.

Sei Whale (pronounced "say" or "sigh")

Balaenoptera borealis
Family: Balaenopteridae

SIZE: Avg adult male 26 ft (8 m), 6 tons. Avg adult female 28 ft (8.5 m), 8 tons. At birth 10 ft (3 m), 1000 lbs.

BODY: Small and sleek. **Head is sharply pointed** with flat rostrum. Up to 285 8 in. long (0.2 m) baleen plates per side ranging from dark gray to yellow. Flippers pointed. Broad flukes. 50-70 short ventral throat grooves. Smallest baleen whale in the N. Pacific.

COLOR: Black or dark steel gray. Light flanks, white belly, and pale streaks on back behind head. **White patch on both flippers.**

DORSAL FIN: Prominent and falcate, located two-thirds distance between head and tail. **Appears simultaneously with blow.**

BLOW: Inconspicuous.

BEHAVIOR: Fast swimmers, may approach boats. Solitary or in groups of 2-3. May breach.

Pieter Folkens

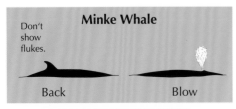

Minke Whale

Don't show flukes.

Back   Blow

CAN BE CONFUSED WITH:

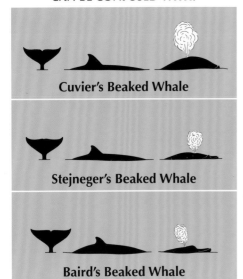

Cuvier's Beaked Whale

Stejneger's Beaked Whale

Baird's Beaked Whale

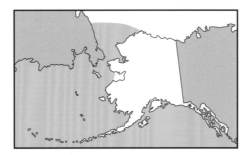

Distribution/Migration: Worldwide. In N. Pacific, found throughout ice-free AK waters in summer. Most spend winters in subtropics (20-25°N).

Mike Munsey

Note pointed rostrum and prominent white patch on flipper of this breaching minke whale.

DIVE PATTERN: 5-8 blows at <1 min intervals between dives up to 20 min long. Arch tail stock high but **don't show flukes.**

HABITAT: Both pelagic and common in bays and shallow coastal waters, often in and near ice.

FOOD HABITS: Prey on variety of schooling fish and zooplankton.

LIFE HISTORY: Sexually mature at 6 yrs. May breed throughout the year. Single calf every 1-2 yrs after gestation of 10-11 mos. Lactation is 6 mos. May live >50 yrs.

STATUS AND HUMAN INTERACTIONS: Status unknown; perhaps 9000 in N. Pacific. Still harvested in parts of Atlantic and Pacific, including Antarctica, for commercial and "scientific" purposes. Incidental capture, vessel collision, and man-made noise are potential threats.

Minke Whale (pronounced "MINK-ee")

Pieter Folkens

SIZE: Avg adult male 46 ft (14 m), 25 tons. Avg adult female 49 ft (15 m), 35 tons. At birth 16 ft (5 m), 2 tons.

BODY: Stocky body with flat, broad head. **Series of fleshy knobs on rostrum and lower lip.** Up to 400 two ft long (0.7 m) dark baleen plates per side and 12-36 ventral throat grooves. **Flippers elongate** (one-third body length) and **flukes broad** with irregular trailing edge.

COLOR: Body black with some white on throat and belly. **Variable amount of white on flippers and flukes.**

DORSAL FIN: Fin small, shape varies (can help distinguish individuals).

BLOW: Broad and bushy, to 10 ft (3 m) high.

BEHAVIOR: Often seen in groups of 2-12 but larger aggregations are common on both winter and summer grounds. **Acrobatic:** breaching, spy-hopping, and lobtailing are common.

Humpback Whale

Fluke Back Blow

CAN BE CONFUSED WITH:

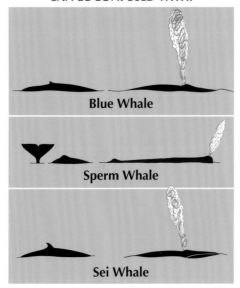

Blue Whale

Sperm Whale

Sei Whale

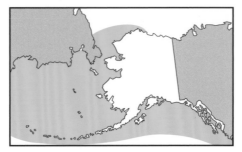

Distribution/Migration: Worldwide. In N. Pacific, migrate from winter breeding grounds in Hawaii, Japan, and Mexico to summer feeding grounds from WA to Chukchi Sea.

UAF/GAP, Permit 1049-1718

Variety of vocalizations including complex songs.

DIVE PATTERN: Blow 4-10 times at 20-30 sec intervals between dives lasting 3-28 mins. **Flukes show prior to deep dives.**

HABITAT: Pelagic and coastal. Feed and breed over shallow banks but may traverse open ocean during migration.

FOOD HABITS: Prey on euphausiids and small schooling fish; some use bubbles to help capture prey.

LIFE HISTORY: Sexually mature at 4-7 yrs. Breed in winter. Single calf born every 1-3 yrs after gestation of 11.5 mos. Lactation lasts 6-10 mos. May live 50 yrs.

STATUS AND HUMAN INTERACTIONS: Endangered. Approx 6-8000 in N. Pacific and increasing. Vulnerable to vessel collision and entanglement in buoyed lines and nets.

Scalloped trailing edge and underside on flukes show before deep dives. Biologists use black and white patterns to recognize individual humpbacks.

Humpback Whale

Pieter Folkens

SIZE: Avg adult 46 ft (14 m), 33 tons. At birth 15 ft (4.5 m), 1100 lbs.

BODY: Body robust. Head profile triangular, upper jaw relatively narrow and arched with up to 180 (to 7 in. long, or 0.2 m) yellow baleen plates per side. **Patches of skin encrusted with barnacles.** 2–7 short throat creases. Flippers paddle-like and pointed. Flukes broad.

COLOR: Mottled gray, some orange patches caused by parasitic whale lice.

DORSAL FIN: No dorsal fin, but a **low hump** followed by several "knuckles" on dorsal ridge of tail stock.

BLOW: Heart-shaped, to 10 ft (3 m) high.

BEHAVIOR: Group size usually 2–3 with large aggregations on feeding and breeding grounds. Breaching and lobtailing common.

DIVE PATTERN: Blow 4–6 times per min between dives of 3–5 min. **Usually raise flukes before a prolonged dive.**

Baird's Beaked Whale

Fluke Back Blow

CAN BE CONFUSED WITH:

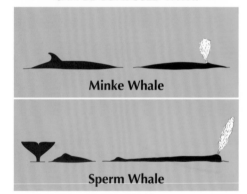

Minke Whale

Sperm Whale

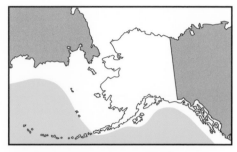

Distribution/Migration: N. Pacific only. Unusual migration pattern. Move s. as far as CA in summer and range as far n. as St. Matthew Is. and the Pribilofs in winter.

HABITAT: Pelagic, generally in waters deeper than 3300 ft.

FOOD HABITS: Feed primarily on squid but also other deep-water species.

LIFE HISTORY: Sexually mature at 8-10 years. Mating occurs in autumn. Single calf every 2-3 yrs born in spring after gestation of 17 mos. May live 70 yrs.

STATUS AND HUMAN INTERACTIONS: Status unknown. Modest historic commercial harvest, currently 10-60 killed annually by Japanese whalers.

©Todd Pusser

Note prominent melon and scarring on backs of tightly grouped Baird's beaked whales. ▶

©Todd Pusser

Note triangular dorsal fin set far aft on back of breaching Baird's beaked whale. ▲

Baird's Beaked (Bottlenose) Whale

Berardius bairdii
Family: Ziphiidae

Cuvier's Beaked (Goosebeak) Whale

Pieter Folkens

SIZE: Avg adult male 20 ft (6 m), 4 tons. Avg adult female 21 ft (6.4 m), 5 tons.

BODY: Robust body. Sloping forehead and short beak. Flippers small and slightly tapered. Tiny median notch between flukes. **One pair of teeth at tip of lower jaw** (do not erupt through gumline in females). One pair of V-shaped throat grooves.

COLOR: Body tan to reddish-brown. **Head and neck white in adults. Scarring common.**

DORSAL FIN: Relatively small, curved, far aft.

BLOW: Inconspicuous and low.

BEHAVIOR: Not frequently seen. Apparently avoid vessels. Travel in pods of 2-15. May breach.

DIVE PATTERN: Deep and long divers. Often a series of shallow surface dives at 20 sec intervals precedes 30 min deep dives. **Forehead breaks surface but**

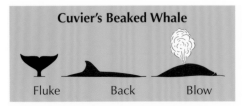

Cuvier's Beaked Whale

Fluke   Back   Blow

CAN BE CONFUSED WITH:

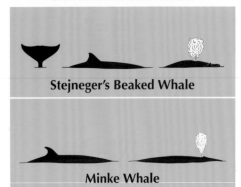

Stejneger's Beaked Whale

Minke Whale

Cuvier's have a sloping forehead, short beak, and short upturned mouthline. Single pair of conical teeth is visible at tip of lower jaw. ▶

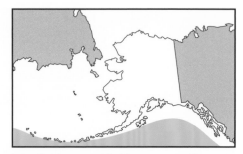

Distribution: Worldwide. In N. Pacific, range north into Gulf of AK and the Aleutians.

©Todd Pusser

beak not usually visible. Show flukes prior to deep dives.

HABITAT: Pelagic. Tropical and temperate waters deeper than 3300 ft.

FOOD HABITS: Poorly known. Thought to eat primarily squid. Deep-water fish as well as benthic invertebrates sometimes taken.

LIFE HISTORY: Poorly known. No marked breeding season. Single calves probably born year-round after unknown gestation period. Solitary strandings are fairly frequent.

STATUS AND HUMAN INTERACTIONS: Status unknown but assumed stable. Possibly 90,000 in e. Pacific. Potential dietary overlap with commercial squid fisheries. Mass mortalities have occurred following military sonar testing.

(pronounced "coo-vee-YAYS")

Cuvier's Beaked (Goosebeak) Whale

Ziphius cavirostris
Family: Ziphiidae

SIZE: Avg adult 16 ft (5 m), 1.3 tons.

BODY: Cylindrical body with small flippers. **Beak long**, well defined. **Lower lips arched near corner of mouth** (most predominantly in males). **One pair teeth large, flattened, triangular** located far back on lower jaw. **Protrude above the gumline in adult males. One pair throat grooves.**

COLOR: Few seen alive. Thought to be gray-brown on the back with lighter belly. Oval and linear scarring common.

DORSAL FIN: Small, curved, far aft.

BLOW: Low and inconspicuous.

BEHAVIOR: Form cohesive groups of 2-15 animals. Often travel abreast and may dive and surface in unison.

DIVE PATTERN: Several shallow, casual dives followed by longer dive of 10-15 min.

Pieter Folkens

Stejneger's Beaked Whale

Fluke   Back   Blow

CAN BE CONFUSED WITH:

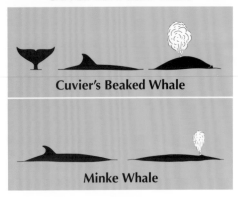

Cuvier's Beaked Whale

Minke Whale

Note scarred body, and single pair of large triangular teeth at corner of mouth in male Stejneger's beaked whale. ▶

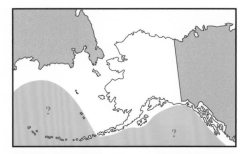

Distribution: N. Pacific only. Probably range from the Pribilofs and Bristol Bay south to Monterey, CA. Known only from strandings, which are most common in the Aleutians and coastal AK.

Kate Wynne

FOOD HABITS: Eat primarily squid but also fish.

HABITAT/LIFE HISTORY/STATUS: Unknown.

Kate Wynne

Skull of whale at left shows inward angle of flattened teeth. Leading edge of both teeth are worn with age.

Stejneger's (Bering Sea) Beaked Whale

Mesoplodon stejnegeri
Family: Ziphiidae

33

SIZE: Avg adult male 26 ft (8 m), 8 tons. Avg adult female 23 ft (7 m), 4 tons. At birth 8 ft (2.4 m), 400 lbs.

BODY: Robust body. Round head with slight beak. Large paddle-like flippers.

COLOR: Striking contrast, black body with white chin, belly, and patch behind eye. Gray "saddle" behind dorsal fin.

DORSAL FIN: Prominent, up to 6 ft tall (2 m) on males, located midway on back. Sexually dimorphic (falcate on females, straight and much taller on males).

BLOW: Bushy, to 10 ft (3 m) high.

BEHAVIOR: Highly social, often travel in pods of 3–40. Acrobatic: breaching, spy-hopping, and lobtailing are common. Often cooperate in hunting and feeding efforts.

DIVE PATTERN: Variable. Many blows at short intervals between dives of 4–10 min.

HABITAT: Coastal waters to 500+ miles offshore.

Pieter Folkens

Transient ♂

Offshore ♂

Resident ♀

Resident ♂

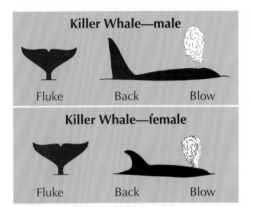

Killer Whale—male

Fluke | Back | Blow

Killer Whale—female

Fluke | Back | Blow

Kate Wynne

Note identical, conical teeth, white eye patch, and short beak of killer whale.

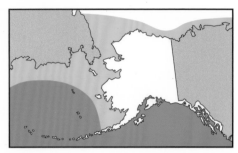

Distribution/Migration: Worldwide. In N. Pacific, transients and year-round residents found in ice-free waters of Gulf of AK, Aleutians, Bering, and Chukchi seas.

Robert Pitman

Note paddle-like flippers and white coloration on this fast-swimming orca.

FOOD HABITS: Most diverse cetacean diet; includes fish, birds, squid, turtles, and marine mammals. Diets of three killer whale ecotypes differ: "residents" eat primarily fish, while "transients" (Bigg's) eat primarily marine mammals. "Offshores" appear to eat large pelagic fish (billfish, sharks). The 3 ecotypes do not interbreed.

LIFE HISTORY: Sexually mature at 10-15 yrs. Mating and birth occur year-round. Single calf every 2+ yrs after gestation of 13-16 mos. Lactation lasts 12+ mos. May live >50 yrs.

STATUS AND HUMAN INTERACTIONS: Resident stocks increasing; transients probably stable or declining. Live-captured for public display in U.S. and Canadian waters until 1977. Compete with some commercial fisheries. As apex predators, accumulate contaminants present in food chain.

Killer Whale (Orca)

Orcinus orca
Family: Delphinidae

Pieter Folkens

SIZE: Avg adult length 7.5 ft (2.3 m), 300 lbs. At birth 3 ft (0.9 m).

BODY: Robust body with **short beak.**

COLOR: Black back and beak with white stripe ("suspenders") from forehead, along ribs to anus. **Light gray** from fore-head **along sides.** Belly white.

DORSAL FIN: Tall, strongly **falcate,** with two-tone color. Forward third dark, trailing two-thirds light.

BLOW: Inconspicuous.

BEHAVIOR: Gregarious, often travel in multi-species herds of tens to several thousand animals. Acrobatic and com-mon bowriders. Fast swimmers.

HABITAT: Mostly pelagic but also occur on continental shelf.

FOOD HABITS: Eat a variety of small schooling fish and squid.

Harbor Seal

Ribbon Seal ♂ ♀

Ringed Seal

Steller
Sea Lion ♂ ♀

Northern Fur Seal ♂ ♀

California
Sea Lion ♂ ♀

Spotted Seal

Bearded Seal

Pacific
Walrus ♂ ♀

Northern
Elephant Seal ♂ ♀

Common Pinnipeds of Alaska

0 1 2 3 FEET
0 .5 1 METER

Lauri Jemison, ADFG, NMFS Permit 358-1564

SIZE: Avg adult male 9 ft (2.7 m), 1500 lbs. Avg adult female 7 ft (2.1 m), 600 lbs. At birth 3 ft (1 m), 45 lbs.

BODY: Robust body; males develop a thickened neck and mane with age. Broad head, bulging eyes, squared snout, and **obvious pinnae.**

COLOR: Dark brown at birth. Adult body **light brown to blond** with dark brown undersides and flippers. Appear **tan** in water.

BEHAVIOR: Gregarious. Gather on haulouts and rookeries. Generally aggressive. Vocalizations are grumbles, growls, and roars but they **do not bark.** May dive to 600 ft (180 m).

HABITAT: Primarily coastal. Use secluded rocky islands for haulouts and rookeries.

FOOD HABITS: Opportunistic. Eat fish, squid, and shrimp. Males fast while holding territories.

Steller Sea Lion

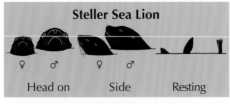

| Head on | Side | Resting |

CAN BE CONFUSED WITH:

California Sea Lion

Northern Fur Seal

Harbor Seal

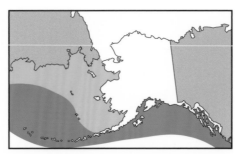

Distribution/Migration: N. Pacific only. In e. N. Pacific, range from s. CA n. through Gulf of AK, Bering Sea, and Aleutians. Seasonal movements common, migration unknown.

Harriet Huber

◄ **Note the differences in profile and color of Steller (light) and California sea lion (dark) in water.**

LIFE HISTORY: Sexually mature at 3-7 yrs. Females breed with dominant males that establish and defend territories for up to 60 days. Single pup per yr born in May-Jul after gestation of 11.5 mos. Lactation lasts 1-3 yrs. Female leaves pup on shore during extended foraging bouts. Females may live 30 yrs. Molting takes place Jul-Nov.

STATUS AND HUMAN INTERACTIONS: Estimated 120,000-140,000 worldwide, approx 93,000 in AK. Endangered but stable w. of 144°W longitude; Threatened and increasing eastward. AK Natives harvest <200/yr for meat and fur. Interactions with commercial fisheries, climate change, marine debris entanglement, and predation by orcas are potential threats.

Steller (Northern) Sea Lion

Eumetopias jubatus
Family: Otariidae

Kim Raum-Suryan, ADFG, NMFS Permit 358-1564

SIZE: Avg adult male 8 ft (2.4 m), 800 lbs. Avg adult female 5 ft (1.5 m), 250 lbs. At birth: 2.6 ft (0.8 m), 13 lbs.

BODY: Sleek body with elongate neck, **tapered snout,** and obvious ear pinnae. Adult males have **prominent sagittal crest** (raised forehead).

COLOR: Medium to **dark brown** when dry, **black when wet.**

BEHAVIOR: Gregarious. Often playful and trained for oceanarium shows. Vocalizations are **dog-like bark,** growl. Fast swimmers (15-20 mph). May dive to 450 ft (137 m) and stay down 20 min but shorter, shallower dives more common. Porpoising common.

HABITAT: Coastal. Remote, sandy island beaches used for rookeries. Haul out on shore, buoys, docks, rafts, etc.

FOOD HABITS: Opportunistic. Eat schooling fish, squid, rockfish, flatfish, hake, salmon, lamprey, dogfish.

California Sea Lion

Head on   Side   Resting

CAN BE CONFUSED WITH:

♀   ♂   ♀   ♂

Steller Sea Lion

♀   ♂   ♀   ♂

Northern Fur Seal

Harbor Seal

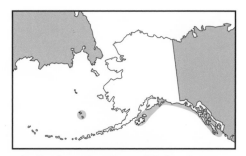

Distribution/Migration: Adult females remain near CA rookeries year-round. Some males move n. in summer-fall after breeding season. Sightings in AK waters are rare but increasing.

Lauri Jemison, ADFG, NMFS Permit 358-1564

LIFE HISTORY: Sexually mature at 6-9 yrs. Single pup per yr born on rookeries in May-Jun after 11.5-mo gestation. Lactation lasts 12 mos. Dominant males hold territories about 30 days and breed polygynously with females within 2-3 wks of pupping. May live 15+ yrs.

STATUS AND HUMAN INTERACTIONS: Increasing, but El Niño conditions periodically reduce pup production and population growth. Estimated 237,000-244,000 from CA to WA. Conflicts with sport fisheries and harbor facilities increase with population growth.

Note difference in forehead profile, size, and color of this lone male California sea lion (dark, in foreground) among a group of Steller sea lions near Dry Bay, AK.

California Sea Lion

Zalophus californianus
Family: Otariidae

Verena A. Gill

SIZE: Avg adult male 6.5 ft (2 m), 300-600 lbs. Avg adult female 4.2 ft (1.3 m), 65-110 lbs. At birth 2 ft (0.6m), 11-12 lbs.

BODY: Small eared seal with **thick fur** and disproportionately **long hind flippers. Ears** tightly rolled and appear to be **located low on neck** (lower than eye level). **Head** round with **large eyes** and **short, conical snout.** Adult males have thickened neck and pronounced **furred crown.**

COLOR: Silver-gray to brown, appear black when wet. Female and juveniles have tan chest and flanks. **Whiskers** black at birth and lighten with age until white by age 6-8 yrs.

BEHAVIOR: Inquisitive and mostly solitary at sea. Adults come ashore only briefly, congregate on rookeries annually to pup and breed. Dive up to 7 min to over 600 ft (180 m). Sleep with nose, one front, and both hind flippers above water ("jughandle" position) while at sea. Porpoising common.

Northern Fur Seal

♀   ♂   ♀   ♂   ⚥

Head on   Side   Resting

CAN BE CONFUSED WITH:

♀   ♂   ♀   ♂

Steller Sea Lion

Harbor Seal

Note dramatic differences in body size and shape between battle-weary territorial male (top) and female fur seals. ▶

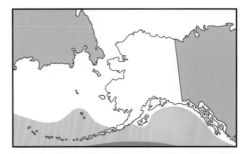

Distribution/Migration: N. Pacific. Long-distance seasonal migrants. Leave AK rookeries in Oct-Nov and remain offshore until Mar-Jun. Adult males overwinter in N. Pacific, females and subadult males spend winter offshore from SE Alaska to CA.

Bruce Robson, ACSNP-TG-ECO, NMFS Permit 1066-1750

HABITAT: Primarily pelagic (7-10 mos per yr). Use remote islands as rookeries (primarily Pribilofs, but also Bogoslof Is., AK, and San Miguel Is., CA).

FOOD HABITS: Feed primarily at night on variety of schooling fish and squid to 10 in. Herring, capelin, pollock, and squid important prey in AK waters.

LIFE HISTORY: Sexually mature at 4-5 yrs. Females breed late Jun-Jul with dominant males that establish and defend territories. Single pups born late Jun-Jul after gestation of 11.8 mos. Lactation lasts 4 mos; pups suckle intermittently between females' foraging trips at sea (up to 250 mi from rookery).

STATUS AND HUMAN INTERACTIONS: Depleted. Approx 700,000 in e. Pacific and declining. Regulated commercial harvest on Pribilofs 1911-1984. Current annual subsistence harvest <800 animals, mostly juvenile males. Debris entanglement, fishery interactions, predation, and climate change are potential threats.

Northern Fur Seal

Callorhinus ursinus
Family: Otariidae

SIZE: Avg adult male 13 ft (3.9 m), 2 tons. Avg adult female 9 ft (2.7 m), 1800 lbs. At birth 3.5 ft (1 m), 65 lbs.

BODY: Largest pinniped in N. Hemisphere. In males, **snout elongate, pendulous,** elephant-like. Broad, **earless,** round head. Nose of females and juveniles **extends slightly beyond mouth.**

COLOR: Pups born black, molt to silver at one mo. Adults are light brown.

BEHAVIOR: Polygynous breeders with social dominance hierarchy. Prevent overheating by flipping wet sand over back with front flippers. Make variety of multipitched cries, snorts, and grunts. Most remain at sea Apr-Dec. May spend 80-90% of this time diving. Deep, long divers with brief surface intervals. Usually dive <20 min to 1500 ft but are known to dive >3000 ft for up to 60 min.

HABITAT: Pelagic when at sea. Sandy CA beaches used for pupping, breeding, molting.

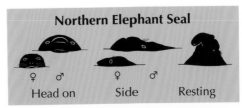

Northern Elephant Seal

♀	♂	♀	♂
Head on		Side	Resting

CAN BE CONFUSED WITH:

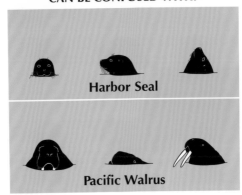

Harbor Seal

Pacific Walrus

Prominent nose extends past mouth even on elephant seal female (L) and juvenile male. ▶

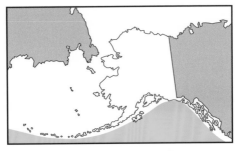

Distribution/Migration: N. Pacific. Long-distance seasonal migrant. Those in AK waters in Apr-Nov are mostly juveniles or adult males. Females remain off WA-OR coast.

Harriet Huber

FOOD HABITS: Fast while on land. At sea, feed on deepwater invertebrates and fish: whiting, ratfish, dogfish, rockfish, squid, octopus.

LIFE HISTORY: Sexually mature at 2-5 yrs. Adults arrive on rookeries Dec-Feb, single pup per yr born in Jan after gestation of 11 mos. Females fast during 28-day lactation and breed before pups are weaned. All return to sea by Feb-Mar. Remain at sea rest of year except during month-long molt (females in Apr-May, males in Jul-Aug).

STATUS AND HUMAN INTERACTIONS: Increasing throughout range. Approx 125,000 in U.S. Commercial harvest in 1800s (for blubber) left only about 100 elephant seals at century's end. Protection has led to steady population increase. Occasionally caught incidentally in offshore fisheries from OR to Aleutians. Increasing frequency of AK sightings and strandings.

Northern Elephant Seal

Kathy Frost

SIZE: Avg adult 5 ft (1.5 m), 150 lbs. At birth 3 ft (1 m), 25 lbs.

BODY: Medium size seal with small head, large eyes, short muzzle. Fur has distinctive **color pattern.**

COLOR: All >1 yr old have **light bands on dark background** encircling the neck, each front flipper, and torso. Background darker on males than females. Pups born with lanugo, molt after 4 weeks to first-year coat of blue-gray back with light sides.

BEHAVIOR: Not wary when hauled out on ice. Run across ice (using alternating front legs, swinging hindquarters) rather than phocidulating like most seals. **Seldom seen in water.** Surface with very little of head showing.

HABITAT: Ice-associated, rarely haul out on land. Southern edge of sea ice winter and spring. Probably pelagic summer and fall.

Ribbon Seal

Head on   Side   Resting

CAN BE CONFUSED WITH:

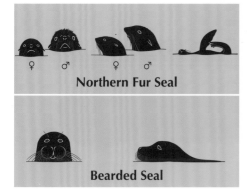

♀   ♂   ♀   ♂

Northern Fur Seal

Bearded Seal

Note low-contrast ribbon pattern on female and white coat of pup. ▶

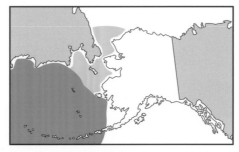

Distribution/Migration: Arctic, N. Pacific. Follow ice: range farther s. in heavy ice (cold) years. Movements in ice-free months uncertain but probably pelagic in Bering and Chukchi seas.

Kathy Frost

FOOD HABITS: Eat a variety of pelagic fish and invertebrates: shrimp, crabs, octopus, squid, cod, sculpin, pollock, capelin, eelpouts.

LIFE HISTORY: Sexually mature at 3-5 yrs. Breed in May. Single pup per yr born early Apr on open ice floes after 11-mo gestation. Lactation is 3-4 wks. Molt annually before ice recedes (Mar-Jul). May live 30 yrs.

STATUS AND HUMAN INTERACTIONS: Status unknown. Estimated 50-100,000 in Bering Sea. Heavy commercial harvest in 1960s by Russian sealers has been reduced to about 4000 per yr. AK Native subsistence harvest of <200 per yr for meat, fur, oil. Vulnerable to reduction in sea ice.

Ribbon Seal

Phoca fasciata
Family: Phocidae

Lloyd Lowry

SIZE: Avg adult 5 ft (1.5 m), 210 lbs. At birth 3 ft (1 m), 26 lbs.

BODY: Medium-size seal with **narrow, dog-like snout.**

COLOR: Dark irregular spots scattered on silver sides and darker back. Pups born with lanugo, molt to adult coat in 3-4 weeks.

BEHAVIOR: Haul out on ice floes late fall to early summer and on land during warmer mos. Often form triads of female, male, and pup during pupping and breeding season. Gregarious at other times. Known to dive to bottom in waters >800 ft (245 m) deep.

HABITAT: Continental shelf to coastal. **Seasonally associated with ice front.** Avoid heavy ice but use floes at ice front fall to summer. In summer, found near shore, on land, and up rivers as well as far offshore.

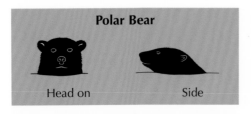

Polar Bear

Head on   Side

Distribution/Migration: Arctic. From Bering Sea into Chukchi and Beaufort seas. Seasonal movement with ice: n. in summer as ice recedes from coast, s. with advancing ice in fall.

© 2012 Joseph Napaaqtuq Sage/AlaskaStock.com

Polar bears rest, mate, give birth, and suckle their young on the ice.

Polar bears dog-paddle with head and much of back above water.

Kathy Frost

FOOD HABITS: Eat primarily ringed and bearded seals. Catch seals mainly by still-hunting at breathing holes, haul-outs, and lairs, or stalking basking seals. Occasionally eat other mammals, eggs, vegetation, beach-cast carrion.

LIFE HISTORY: Sexually mature at 4-8 yrs. Breed polygamously Apr-Jun. 1-3 cubs every 28 mos. Pregnant females dig a den Oct-Dec where cubs are born Dec-Jan and stay until Mar-Apr. Lactation lasts 28 mos. May live to 25-30 yrs.

STATUS AND HUMAN INTERACTION: Population apparently healthy. Approx 3-4000 in AK. Sport hunters killed approx 200 per yr from 1940s until banned in 1972. Subsistence use (for hide, meat, handicraft) by AK Natives <100 per yr. Loss of sea ice threatens denning and foraging of this ice-dependent species.

Polar Bear

Ursus maritimus
Family: Ursidae

SIZE: Avg adult male 5 ft (1.5 m), 70 lbs. Avg adult female 4 ft (1.2 m), 60 lbs. At birth 10 in (0.3 m), 5 lbs.

BODY: Largest member of the weasel family, smallest marine mammal. **Long, flat tail** and webbed hind feet. Retractable claws on front paws. Head round with **small eyes, triangular nose, and visible ear pinnae.** Densest fur of any mammal (no blubber).

COLOR: Body dark brown to blond with lighter head. Head and neck lighten with age until **white** in **old** animals.

BEHAVIOR: Usually swim on back with feet in the air but may swim on stomach, porpoise, and roll repeatedly while traveling. Groom fur frequently. Eat only while floating. Groom, rest, and nurse young while floating or hauled out on rocky shores or sandbars. Front paws used for foraging and grooming but not swimming. Form sex-segregated groups. Hundreds may float together in "raft."

Kate Wynne

Sea Otter

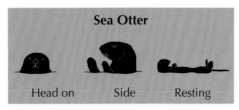

Head on   Side   Resting

CAN BE CONFUSED WITH:

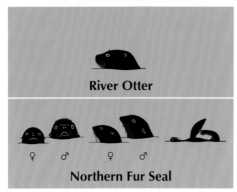

River Otter

♀   ♂   ♀   ♂

Northern Fur Seal

Young sea otter pups are so buoyant they are unable to submerge. The mother may swim with the pup on her chest for months. ▶

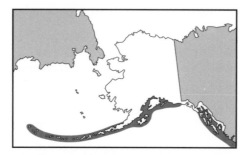

Distribution/Migration: N. Pacific. AK population ranges from Aleutians to Prince William Sound and SE AK. Non-migratory but move in response to prey abundance.

© 2012 Lon Lauber/AlaskaStock.com

while resting. Short and shallow divers, usually <100 ft for 1-2 min.

HABITAT: Coastal. Shallow waters with rocky or sandy substrate.

FOOD HABITS: Eat primarily benthic invertebrates: clams, mussels, urchins, crabs, fish. Capable of dramatically affecting size and abundance of prey.

LIFE HISTORY: Sexually mature at 3-6 yrs. Peak breeding Sep-Oct in AK. Single pup per 1+ yrs after variable gestation of 5-8 mos. In AK, most pups born in May (on land or water) and are dependent on mother for 5-12 mos.

STATUS AND HUMAN INTERACTIONS: Approx 80,000 in AK waters. Numbers increasing in SE and SC AK, but listed as threatened in SW AK due to drastic declines in the Aleutians. Subsistence and handicraft use of pelts by AK Natives. Vulnerable to oil contamination and boat strikes. Known to compete with shellfisheries and to entangle in coastal gillnets.

The following terms are defined as they are used in this book.

Amphibious: Lives both on land and in water.

Amphipod: Small crustacean with laterally compressed body, in the order Amphipoda.

Baleen: Bony material formed into comb-like plates, grows from upper jaw of mysticete whales.

Benthic: Associated with the ocean bottom.

Blow: Moist air forcefully exhaled from lungs and through the blowhole of a surfacing cetacean.

Bowride: Swim in the wake created by a moving boat, often at the bow or front of the boat.

Breach: Jump clear of the water surface.

Carnivore: Flesh eater, member of the taxonomic order Carnivora.

Cetacean: Whale, dolphin, or porpoise; member of the order Cetacea.

Chevron: V-shaped stripes.

Coastal: Waters adjacent to coastline.

Copepod: Small crustacean in the class Copepoda.

Depleted Status: Species whose numbers are below its optimal sustainable population level.

Dimorphism: Two different forms or traits. Sexual dimorphism: traits differ between sexes.

Dive pattern: Typical pattern and timing of a whale's blows and dives.

Echolocation: Means of locating prey and other objects by generating and receiving sound signals (sonar).

Endangered Status: Species in danger of extinction in all or a significant portion of its range.

Euphausiid: Small shrimp-like crustacean in the order Euphausiacea. Also called krill.

Falcate: Strongly curved or hooked.

Fissiped: "Split-footed" carnivores, including weasels, bears, cats, dogs, and raccoons; members of the suborder Fissipedia, order Carnivora.

Fluke: Flat propelling surface of cetacean tail (see p. 6).

Gestation: Carrying young in the uterus until delivery.

Haul out (verb): To rest onshore.

Haulout (noun): Shoreside resting site.

Lactation: Production of milk by female; duration of suckling.

Lair: Den

Lanugo: Long white fur retained by some seal pups after birth.

Lobtail: Slap water surface with tail.

Melon: Bulbous forehead of toothed

whales; contains nasal passages and fat (see p. 6).

Molt: Shedding and replacing fur.

Monogamous: One male mates with one female.

Morphology: Body form, shape, or structure.

Opportunist: Eats a variety of prey, usually what is most easily accessible.

Pack Ice: Mass of broken ice pieces, at edge of permanent sea ice.

Pelagic: Associated with deep, open water.

Phocidulate: Move by undulating or heaving the body in a caterpillar-like manner.

Pinna: External ear flap (plural: pinnae).

Pinniped: "Fin-footed" carnivores, including seals, sea lions, and walrus: members of the suborder Pinnipedia, order Carnivora.

Piscivore: Fish eater.

Pod: Group of cetaceans traveling together.

Polygynous: One male mates with more than one female.

Porpoising: Non-cetacean behavior of breaking water surface while swimming fast.

Quadrupedal: Four-legged mobility.

Rookery: Haulout used by pinnipeds for pupping and breeding.

Rostrum: Upper jaw (see p. 6).

Sexual maturity: Age at which animal is first capable of breeding.

Spatulate: Broad, flat, round shape.

Specialist: Eats a limited number of prey species.

Spyhop: Poke head vertically out of the water.

Taxonomy: Classification of organisms according to how they are related to one another.

Threatened Status: Species likely to become endangered within foreseeable future in all or significant portion of its range.

Zooplankton: Minute animals adrift in water column, including early life stages of fish and invertebrates. Includes copepods and amphipods.

Abbreviations

approx	approximately
avg	average
e.	east or eastern
ft	foot or feet
hr	hour
in.	inches
lb	pound
m	meter
max	maximum
min	minute
mo	month
mph	miles per hour
n.	north or northern
s.	south or southern
sec	seconds
w.	west or western
wt	weight
yr	year
♀	female
♂	male
<	less than
>	greater than

PAGE	English (common)	Latin (scientific)	Japanese	Russian	Alaska Native

CETACEANS

Mysticetes

8	Bowhead whale	*Balaena mysticetus*	hokkyoku kujira	grendlandskiy	agyaax̂[1], agviq[3]
10	North Pacific right whale	*Eubalaena japonica*	semi kujira	yuzhnyy kit	kulumax̂[1]
12	Blue whale	*Balaenoptera musculus*	shiro nagasu kujira		umĝulix̂[1]
14	Fin whale	*Balaenoptera physalus*	nagasu kujira	finval	mangidax̂[1]
16	Sei whale	*Balaenoptera borealis*	iwashi kujira	seyval	alamax̂chx̂ix̂[1]
18	Minke whale	*Balaenoptera acutorostrata*	koiwashi kujira	zalivov, minke	agamaxchix̂[1]
20	Humpback whale	*Megaptera novaeangliae*	zato kujira	gorbach	alamax̂[1]
22	Gray whale	*Eschrichtius robustus*	koku kujira	seryy kit	chickakhluk[6]

Odontocetes

24	Sperm whale	*Physeter macrocephalus*	makko kujira	kashalot	agdaxx̂ix̂[1]
26	Beluga	*Delphinapterus leucas*	shiro iruka	belukha	alam quhmaa[1], sisuaq[3]
28	Baird's beaked (bottlenose) whale	*Berardius bairdii*	tsuchi kujira	severnyy plavun	chiidux̂[1]
30	Cuvier's beaked (goosebeak) whale	*Ziphius cavirostris*	akabo kujira	kyuv'erov	chumchugagakh[6]
32	Stejneger's (Bering Sea) beaked whale	*Mesoplodon stejnegeri*	ogiha kujira	remnezub Stegnegera	kigan agaliusiak[6]
34	Killer whale (orca)	*Orcinus orca*	shachi	kosatka	aglux̂[1]
36	Pacific white-sided dolphin	*Lagenorhynchus obliquidens*	kama iruka	belobokii delfin	
38	Dall's porpoise	*Phocoenoides dalli*	rikuzen iruka	belokrylka	kdangix̂[1]
40	Harbor porpoise	*Phocoena phocoena*	nezumi iruka	morskaja svinya	alaadax̂[1]

PAGE	English (common)	Latin (scientific)	Japanese	Russian	Alaska Native
PINNIPEDS					
Otariids					
46	Steller (northern) sea lion	*Eumetopias jubatus*	todo	sivuch	qawax̂[1], uginaq[2], taan[4], wiinaq[5]
48	California sea lion	*Zalophus californianus*	kariforunia ashika	morskoi lev	
50	Northern fur seal	*Callorhinus ursinus*	kita ottosei	severhyi morski kotik	laqudax̂[1], aataak[2]
Phocids					
52	Northern elephant seal	*Mirounga angustirostris*	kita zou azarashi	morski slon	
54	Bearded seal	*Erignathus barbatus*	agohige-azarashi	morski zayatz (lakhtak)	mukluk[2], ugruk[3]
56	Harbor seal	*Phoca vitulina*	gomafu-azarashi	obykhovennyi tyulen	isuĝix̂[1], tsaa[4], tsuwiq[5]
58	Ribbon seal	*Phoca fasciata*	kurakake-azarashi	polosatyi tyulen (krylatka)	qasruliq[2], quigulik[3]
60	Spotted (largha) seal	*Phoca largha*	komimi-azarashi	larga	ukutux̂[1], issuriq[2], qasigiaq[3]
62	Ringed seal	*Pusa hispida*	fuiri-azarashi	kolchataya nerpa (akiba)	nayiq[2], natchiq[3]
Odobenid					
64	Pacific walrus	*Odobenus rosmarus*	seiuchi	morzh	amgaadax̂[1], asveq[2], aiviq[3]
MARINE FISSIPEDS					
68	Polar bear	*Ursus maritimus*	shiro kuma	belyi medved	kdam tanĝaaĝa[1], arlunaq[2], nanuq[3]
70	Sea otter	*Enhydra lutris*	rakko	morskaya vydra	chngatux̂[1], aarnaq[2], yùxwch´[4]

Alaska Native: 1 = Unangax̂ (western Aleutians and Pribilof Aleut), 2 = Yup'ik, 3 = Inupiat, 4 = Tlingit, 5 = Alutiiq, 6 = Aleut